5.00

AF893595

# HANDS

# HANDS

Jean Monahan

*1991 Anhinga Prize for Poetry*
*Selected by Donald Hall*

Anhinga Press . Tallahassee, Florida . 1992

# Acknowledgements

Grateful acknowledgement is made to the following publications in which versions of these poems previously appeared:

Big Wednesday: "A Letter to Robin Silverman"

The New Republic: "The Bones of Potter's Field"

Shenandoah: "Followed by Children Who Threw Stones"

The Webster Review: "The Way the Yellow," "O Orange Cat Do Your Chameleon Act," and "The Voice of Thy Brother's Blood"

Grolier Contest (1988): "Digging" and "Mrs. Leonard Works in Her Garden"

~

Published by Anhinga Press, Inc., Tallahassee, Florida.

Copyright ©1992 by Jean Monahan.
All rights reserved.
Printed in the United States of America.

Monahan, Jean.
Hands.

(The Anhinga Prize for Poetry 1991)
I. Title. II. Series: Anhinga Poetry Prize Series.

Library of Congress Card Number 92-070093
ISBN 0-938078-34-8

~

Cover art and design by Judith Porter.
Book design by Geoffrey Brock.
Production coordinator: Maureen Rogers.

~

Anhinga Press thanks the following for help in selecting finalists from 325 entries: Heidi Altman, Brant Brock, Frances Brock, Geoffrey Brock, Bill Brubaker, Rick Campbell, Donald Caswell, Robert Coutré, Meri Culp, Janet Heller, Steven Huss, Andrea Kelly, P.V. LeForge, Molly Mabe, Doug Martin, Elsie Rogers, Maureen Rogers, Mary Jane Ryals, Stephanie Sgouros, Elaine Smith, Gabriele Stauf, Alison Watkins, and especially the initial coordinator Julie Weiler.

*For Betsy*
*and for my family,*

*with great thanks to Van K. Brock and Donald Hall,*
*Judith Porter and Melissa Zieve,*
*and to Zhou Shi Zhong,*
*who helped me translate the two*
*classical Chinese poems that appear in this book.*

# Contents

## *I. Smiling as She Offers Her Awful Gift*



## *II. A Letter to Robin Silverman*

## *III. Followed by Children Who Threw Stones*

*Smiling as She Offers Her Awful Gift*

# Showing the Heart

With the gratified patience of a tortured saint
my brother bows and opens his shirt
to reveal how skinny
only he can be. Neatly
boxed as a Chinese kite
his slight chest arcs in delicate
waves, ribs bellied with the wind that sustains
him. In a tender corner below
the left nipple his boy's heart jumps
like a trapped devil, angrier still as we elbow
near to squelch his pulse
against our fingertips.

~

The boy before me points, his arm a slow arrow
aimed at my heart. Below, three buttonholes
have unwed their buttons, my blouse
burst open at the neck. Where he expected
lace, the first false curve
of a padded cup, the line of my t-shirt
scoops my chest. Quickly I hunch
and correct the buttons. They sweat in my pinch,
shy away from each noose.

~

In the spring of her first year of teaching,
Sister Ellen introduces the most important organ.
Bypassing the chapter in the teacher's book, we
dissect the heart in oral report, home-
made versions of the flood and gates. She
brings diagrams, movies, but the class remains
overcocky, restless, more sure than anyone else
of our own miraculous biology. On the last day she brings
us a real deer heart, stashed in a cooler
below her desk. *Notice how much smaller*,
she remarks, gently unfolding the white butcher's wax
where it bleeds in her palm like a crushed fruit.
Around the room she walks,
smiling as she offers her awful gift.

# Magdalene

Since the day of your death
I have gone about like a young widow
who has wrapped up her still-beautiful flesh
to mourn, my breasts bound with your winding-cloth.
I have been faithful, though you refused
my body I would have given freely
to your large hands and gentle eyes.

*When you moved beyond me in the pinching mob*
*you grasped like a lover all the waving arms,*
*the rows of pink and green palms thrashing.*

Too late, now, for Jerusalem's forgiveness,
though alone among your followers I wept
at your knees, broke open my box of spikenard
to wash your feet. No one will believe
you revealed yourself to me first.
I am only the woman whose wet hair
was a luxury you allowed yourself.

*I could shed this body that binds me to earth,*
*rise up, with you, before the rising sun.*
*Master, if you love me, save me. Touch.*

# A Triolet for Lorelei

Sailor, the song swelling my lungs
can only be heard by you.
Though the air thrums with a hundred white wings,
listen to the song that swells in my lungs:
like the peal of a bell repeatedly rung,
lusty as the crooning of the midnight crew,
the words billowing my lungs
are meant only for you.

I'll smile and part my hair like a veil
to show you my body of glossy foam.
As you race to hoist the topmost sails,
the wind dishevels my veil
and smiling, you turn and know you have failed:
the rocks of my island look suddenly like home
when I part my hair like a veil
and show you my body of glossy foam.

Never look back at what you leave behind,
but rest your head in my sparkling arms.
I will rub your temples with tingling brine
until you forget all you have left behind—
free as the fish, graceful and blind,
to sheer with the waves or doze like a clam.
Did you think you could leave me behind
when I held your head in my sparkling arms?

# The Girl by Green River

*after Rexroth's translation of the anonymous Sixth Dynasty poem*

When I stopped there for water,
hearing my voice creak down the well of my throat
dry as an empty bucket,
the same wind that jostled my heels up the path
set leaves to dance in the muddy grass.
It was a small house, a few steps from the bridge,
and softly I knocked.

A young girl, not more than fifteen, swung
back the bamboo door. Smoke billowed and lingered
by the open window, a smell of fish and charred
pine. She merely lifted her eyes to mine,
did not flutter a glance toward the darkening ground
but held my own stare steadily. She brought water
in a cool bowl, but would not sit.

*Where is your husband?* I asked
and watched for the blush in her pale skin.
She answered plainly, *I have none. This house*
*was my father's before he died. He had no sons.*
*It is mine.* I drank slowly, letting the cold
stream and bind my thirst. She wore her hair
pinned back, like a woman; a boyish set to her mouth:
half-frown, half-pout. Not beautiful, but sturdy,
and when she moved to fill my bowl again her young smell
rose and soothed me. I would like to remember
more of her hands, but she kept them hidden in her sleeves.

When I could drink no more
and think of no more questions to detain her,
she smiled and bowed and unlatched the door.
Willows waved and kneeled in the river. I stood higher
than her house in fifty steps, the bank firm
and the path rising. As I turned, once,
I caught sight of her form: she stood on the bridge,
back straight, sleeves pushed up, and lowered,
one by one, fresh traps into the water.

## Home Movies

When I first see her, hair like twisted kelp
down her long knobbed spine, she is at the sea-
side. It is all new: the rhythmic shatter of
the waves, the odd way the earth digs and cups
the heels, slows the steps, grits the arches
whether she runs or walks. How the salty smell
of rotting, the hot squeeze of the sun, let her go
only at night: sticky, itchy, tired. And always
the monstrous baying of the invisible seahound.

Soon she is ballerina, mermaid, seal. The dark
green light off the sea has stained her body teak.
She wants to float, buoy-light, in the cove, flop
down rich and scattered as the foam. Nothing deters
her, not the laughter, not her father's camera.
When she tires of salt she stands up, walks the
hard sand where the waves rush least. Shells
and horseshoe crabs equally delay, pull her hair
about her ears as she jackknifes in place and stares.

The gathered gray in the clouds overhead is
partly filter, partly screen. One gull plows a
rolling furrow. Could anyone have been so stupid,
danced with that monkey grin under this hot white
light? Wall-less, broken, the boathouse exposes
itself in the distance. I've tried but its rusted
heart won't start. Wood drifts and nods in the
shifting wash. Though I am sick of her already,
something gripping drags my footsteps.

# Perseus Appears to the Three Gray Women

What a different world it might have been
were it not for the man

who stepped out of the wind
shaped the way our dreams had always shaped him.

What hues might have blazed, if not for his fire-
colored cloak and bronze shield, charcoal hair

and copper skin? We remember now his smile,
curling up, smoke thin, from the lid of a scowl,

how he watched us watch him, all the while
gauging our hands, as we passed our one eye

beneath our gray wings. The exact moment we lost
sight of him remains uncertain; under the pregnant

clouds that impound our land there is only this
sudden, heartsick wonder: in a careless

moment one might blindly trade
the world into a stranger's hand.

# Putting the Hand Out

When Thomas put his hand out to touch
the hands of Jesus, press his clouded
fingernails in the marks the other nails made,
he did so as a child deaf since birth
shapes his hand around the mouths of others
to hear words; insisting as a child would
that a wound must be seen to be believed.

My father rolls his shirt up with feeble
fingers, reveals the neat, flat "I" of a scar
blazoned like a slogan over his heart.
New spirit entered through this letter
that the pump, brutish muscle, might continue.
Not faith but fear makes the wound real.
It was easier to believe than see.

# Bipassages

On the night before his heart is bypassed
with four new locks (the surgeon's needle
a gondolier pole dipped in living canals)
I call my father, run my fingers over
the numbers to the hospital. He asks
if I need anything, when did we talk last,
the peevish static which joins us priestly
and unenlightened, waiting for a full
confession. His voice takes on the timbre
of my younger brother's, the hiker
with the bad knee who walked from Maine
to Georgia on the Appalachian spine.
*Stop it, Kevin,*

I almost say, *I know you're afraid.*
But we tangle our lines a moment longer,
let random thoughts report. When he pauses,
Kevin's arm clings tighter to the pumped-up
tire we float on in the lake: the biggest tire
we always wanted for ourselves, wanted
without the other. I will push him
off, pound him if he doesn't let go.
But he only frowns and perseveres,
bumps the patchy craft against the rocks.
*Nothing to be concerned about,*
my father says, *I'll be under*
*five hours. Out-of-touch for two days.*

# Commandments

My first piece of jewelry was a bracelet
of flat, square links and snap-on charms;
ten scrolls engraved with the ten commandments,
hammered on cheap yellow metal. Wet,
it had the salty tang of green tomatoes: their metallic
bite when plucked from the vine, the stench
of the seeds against the vegetable knife.
More than the words, the shape of the scrolls
caught my eye: ten bright flecks reflecting
nothing but light.

~

Later, *covet*, that ancient word, lodged
in my mouth like a peach pit. Summers, my brothers and I
gathered around the neighbor's pool
but the water was rarely clean and by mid-June
red and black berries from overhanging trees
bobbed and rotted in the chlorine. It became
the neighborhood bathtub; twigs and leaves
nudged like soap; until, one day, live fish
were dropped into the blue. A few
even managed to live briefly, helpless
lungs opening, folding.

~

As a child I coveted
all I saw and heard: dust raging in a sunslit,
the fragrance creased into my mother's dress.
This was the appetite of a lifetime,
relentless, serious. Once, noses pressed
against a department store window of cut-glass bowls
and vases, *Choose one*, she whispered, eyeing
the imitation Waterford. But the loveliest snaked up,
unmistakable: violet-blue, one long curve.
At home she frowned. *Didn't you know it was colored*
*water?* She turned from the sink to where I stood
transfixed. Magic drained in a steady gush,
a color like blueberry juice washed from the glass.

# O Orange Cat, Do Your Chameleon Act

O orange cat, do your chameleon act,

divulge from the arm of the chair
your orange bag of tricks and kinks:

slip on your cape of marmalade aspic,
orange-peel flecks spiraling

from shoulders to shins; next,
let paws dissolve to lily pads,

ears fold over and sprout wings.
Little sphinx, knickknack,

always on the verge or just
fresh from a nap. Fir-green

eyes, innocent as pears,
glow in your head like stone

eyes on a buddha. Distilling
in white sun you sing

a cleaning song,
starting with four pin cushions

amber and pink, your sculling tongue:
salmon boat parting waves of wheat.

You are never quite complete.
Your stealthy stroll along the shelf

a leopard who fells the elusive sunspill
or lion who taunts the tiger lily.

Late at night, you curl like a slug
in the whorl of my sheets, already asleep

when I turn out the lights.
We go off this way together:

I never remember the point of separation.
i straggle out on all fours as you

rise above me, giant legs like jack's
beanstalk. i put my hands up

to reach you and ten hooks appear.
Hoisted to your shoulder, the earth

pitches below in raggedy squares;
my claws stitch your skin to my fear.

i can't remember any other way
of embracing. i lean into the crook

of your arm, fray a patch along your
chin, slit both eyes and start to purr.

# Pianissimo

The day my brother lost his finger
(he and his friend yukked it up out back,
slipped the blade of the shears through the hedges,
the digit no bigger than a twig
finally found) I sat down
at the piano and played my lesson
through twice, perfectly, without making
a sound.

# The Voice of Thy Brother's Blood

*And the Lord said unto Cain, Where is Abel thy brother?*
*And he said, I know not: Am I my brother's keeper?*
*And he said, What hast thou done? the voice*
*of thy brother's blood crieth unto me from the ground.*
— Genesis 4:9, 4:10

1 Before you speak, look at my hands.
See the muscles curled like snakes
around each knuckle? These are mighty
tools; with them I plow, rake, spread
the earth with herded dung. At night
they hang like wood from the ends
of my arms. In dreams they crawl
up my chest, wrap around my throat;
they are my enemy, the voice
of my brother's blood.

2 Most mornings we rose and ate by firelight.
Mother pounded corn into flat, cooked cakes,
filled our hands with almonds and grapes.
To Father she gave wine, apricots.
We'd ride East, driving the sheep before us
until the sun shone high overhead. In
a shady place we'd eat and sleep. Sometimes
Abel and I'd stay awake and make up stories:
about doves, why they don't sing, or about
things like locusts, what it means
when they come. Abel believed everything
I said. One summer near the tent we dug a well,
patting mud over mud and fitting the stones.
Abel worked slowly, making sounds under
his breath like a bird. Father watched
our work, not saying a word.

3 When we were 20 and 21
Abel worked the hills and pens
and I kept the northern fields.
One day my father said, *The time*

*has come. We have harvested well.*
*Now let us offer the Creator all*
*that is good, the best of our yield.*

On a wood altar Abel piled fattened ewes;
I went after, laying on fruit and sheaves
of wheat. We prayed for acceptance,
at a distance. By dawn a mound
of wheat remained; figs and berries blew
in the dust; the ribs of one sheep,
found under a bush, were gnawed
and marked by giant teeth.

4 Father wept. He often did:
I never understood why.
He lay near the altar and chanted.
The few words we heard — *sweat*
and *bread* — confused us further.
We tried to comfort him but he pushed
us away, his red face streaked with dirt.
At last he explained: *By this we may see*
*as Yahweh sees: he has eaten*
*only what pleases him.*

5 Small white burns parched my lips;
my ears gone sick with a terrible singing.
I could not look at my father's face
so I looked at my hands, counting blisters.
Unable to look I went out from that place:
I would throw myself from a ledge,
bury my heart in the soil. I would
go willingly to a viper's kiss:
I licked my lips in anticipation.
Abel came running after, calling
and calling my name.

6 He should not have come.
Who knows the mind under that white sun?
I could not bear his pity, the perfect
tears welling and rolling, his bleating
tongue. I pushed him back against a rock
and left him there to sleep it off.

7 When ever did I not believe nor
do your bidding? In one evil hour
I ruined three men. I walked West, Father,
to a place of elms and great lilies.
Just up to the edge. Not one bird moved.
Black vines barred the dense border.
A lazy slither in the leaves
and I fell to my knees; I knew
everything then.

8 Mother saw me first, gagging a scream
in her shawls. Abel lay near her,
deaf with fever. His eyes strayed
from mine when I leaned to touch him.
Before I could speak he shuddered
and finished. *Were you not with him?*
*Was he pushed? Did he leap?* No
answer came and then, from every furrow,
his inarticulate shriek.

9 Enoch is a good son; he sticks close
to the woman and minds her. I live
with them when I can, teaching Enoch
the ways of the land. But when a black-
ness comes, like thunder in my head,
I go out into this land of Nod,
where we live, and eat only bread,
a little water. I see things: my father's
tired head, my tired hands; I hear things:
my mother's scream, my brother's blood.

10 I don't make up stories anymore.
Around the city I've built, soil is rocky
to the north but fertile to the south.
When one of my herd dies I leave it lie
for the preying beasts. I've never
had locusts, but when I look real close,
square small dents, mice teeth maybe,
mark the stalks of corn and wheat.

*A Letter to Robin Silverman*

# Origin

The moon rose early
every night that week, a wafer half-
buried in the deepening blue
(the way lady slippers loaf

in the silt
of tidal pools) so
we rose early, also,

to watch mist brush the manes of the giant dunes,
dredged awake by a heron's whoop
as she circled, outstretched, over our cabin roof.

Drawn unresisting into the sea's cool berth
our bodies softened, brine's sheen over all
our features. But not until

the night we stood, knees gently folded
in the waves' black crease,
did we release,

by silver light, our former shapes: your spine,
when you dove, fanning to a marlin's fin,
our legs reseamed for watery locomotion,

hair sleek as sealskin: briefly plunged
into that state of grace before the spit curl left us
beached. Homeward bound, the dunes

like silent sand whales drifting beneath our
movement, a forgotten madrigal of water
and mammal still rolled in our ears:
mournful, undecipherable, half-familiar.

## Overcast

Slate-black clouds stockpile above the valley
schoolhouse, crumpling overhead like bolts
of seersucker. Weather is the star

attraction in Montpelier: the most dazzling arc
when sun and rain, like two acrobats,
tumble and swap under a white tent. I am

grateful to be alone. I left my family
a mile down the road, noisily adjusting
their chairs in front of my brother's house;

slipped out before my lover could wonder whether
to join or stay. Rigid and shiny, the lawn chairs
have borne, with true Vermont stoicism, the weight

of the long weekend: have kept us all upright
and uncomfortable, afternoons into interminable night
falls, when we pull, without fail, our chairs

in a circle. Round and round the conversations circled,
turned on a silent question. And still, no sign
I'll join my life with his, no vow we'll live

with the other's needs. By now they must have gone
inside and set the first twigs of a fire roaring.
Out here, there's nothing to bring in when it rains:

cows never bother to tuck their heads, but,
in a downpour, sink to their knees, to meditate
until it is over. I admire their grace, that

ease of surrender. Maybe lowing is a kind of prayer.
When they saunter in pairs up their private slopes
it's because I have come too near: their only fear

the smell of a stranger. By now I've reached
the bridge that fords Blue Creek; rain dents
the water as it flows downstream, making it flash dully

as a hammered shield. Built into the left embankment
are a pair of houses, their bottom boards a few feet
above water. Together they sag, a single creature:

rusted eaves curled up like wings, porches homely
as gap-toothed grins. Swallows zig-zag
in and out of the upper windows, then ride

a wind-chute beneath the bridge. Ushered in
on the breeze are smells of the field: violets beheaded
in a sudden tail flick, apples "off-the-tree,"

limestone and manure heaped behind barns. How strange
not to have recognized the smell of his fear,
wholesome and acrid as my own. Above Blue Creek,

two houses find support in each other's peril.
When I get home I'll tell them love,
even marriage, is possible.

# Rehearsing the Amaryllis

Earth releases his humid grip and breaks
the brown crumble of her slumber;
her waist, pale and plump
as a melon, a bulging full moon
in his fingers. Only her yellow-green
leaves are exposed, those startling banners
nipped into triangles. She waves
them in the face of Day,
whose attention wavers.

On a morning the windows are fitted with sun skin,
buds appear to pucker on the stem,
slow mouths opening
to a song. All night she trolls,
notes oozing up like spring
from her roots. Earth can hardly contain
such mirth, her round
weight held in his palm.

The next week she smiles
and reveals two teeth, dull
yellow stamen. He can almost hear them sharpen
on the air the mouths suck in.
She pulls her face
away from his, lips curling
back like victrolas ready
for the music.

Sounds, ruddy and gorgeous,
trumpet from bloodred openings;
this is the lovesong of bulb
and soil; the valentine
they've made of one
another.        Amaryllis

lets her first bloom drop, purple
as a tongue after a boysenberry:  there is little
time left.  Before the moon
has scaled the clouds
he tips her lusty throat and makes her sing
into his mouth.

## Biking at Dusk along the Charles

At this hour, this late in summer,
night air sweats with a pulpy chill.
The sky hews open like a ripe-bellied melon,
tender, juiceslick seeds overrunning
the teablack edges of the eastern half.
Above the glinting pedals, my knees
paddle the air's whitewater: every muscle
hunched to a quiver, my quick breath
spiced with the new-mown grass. The river
shifts its mood toward sleep, collects
under bridges and curls against banks,
wanly indulgent of the loose-knit boats
that slap and moan into its mossy shanks.
I gather speed with the dying light,
warming to my own heat as I turn and leave
the river. Cattails sough
with wading wind. The moon unknots
her silk bedgown and softly slips
down amongst men.

# In Memory of Ching Erh

*translation of Li Bai*

Low notes choke in a flute.

Ching Erh wakes from her dream to the moon rocking
above her roof,

rocking, boatlike, above her roof.

Greensheathed willows have withered to yellow

beside the Ba River since last I saw you.

On the plains of the Lu Yu, I toast the autumn moon.

On the old road to Xian Yang, dust and noise have
settled down,

dust and noise have settled down.

Winds from the west, the bloodstained sun,

brush the grassy walls of the Han tombs.

# An Old Poem to Yuan Wei-zhi

*translation of Hsueh T'ao*

My verse uses sounds common to all poets,

but I alone know their subtler tones.

I sing of flowers bleached by moonlight,

lament the drenched willows in my morning poems.

Faithfully, I hide my heart's green jade,

write freely of love on peony-embossed sheets.

Helpless, aging, alone, life eludes my hold.

Let me live to keep you in full bloom.

# Mrs. Leonard Works in Her Garden

Bright star of the yard's blearing horizon
Mrs. Leonard, 73, works in her garden.
A leaf of sky has fluttered loose,
and landed, all of a piece,

in the shape of her dress, a fierce
and unsunny blue against which
her arms brush like clouds. Birth
is what she wrests, why, in the subtle hush

summoning dark, she delivers from exhausted,
late August haunches offspring red,
butteryellow, summergreen, her knees planting hard
asexual kisses on the cool reluctance

of the earth's mouth. The geraniums grow rakish
with the onset of evening, their clusters drenched
with a female smell: she clears the dead
petals that litter their beds. Up in high,

leafy towers, emerald-gowned Rapunzels give
their hair to the wind. Of these she saves
the plump and flaxen, for the largest pot
that sits in her kitchen. Already the night

things creep and root as she carries the light,
a single gold crescent, crooked in her arms;
thorough, almost thoughtful as they eat,
know, too, how soon the sweet fruit falls.

# Victorian Woman Spies Her Suitor in Her Looking Glass

*a reply to Nemerov's "I Only Am Escaped Alone To Tell Thee"*

Lover, you breathe like a hooked fish
in the nervous dark of my front hall
as I stand before the silver lake
that swallows the house from the opposite wall.
The banister, humped as a coral reef,
hangs out-of-reach from where I float;
when I turn my head, the gas lamp
threads, like a school of fish,
in and out of its rails.

Yes, I can feel you watching
my nightly swim into my own reflection
though the glass refuses to show
my chignon loosed into waves, the scaled
eyelets of my corset unhooked, my ribs
imprinted with gills of lace.
Skittish crab in your inky corner,
I see you knuckle your mouth
into silence, afraid to watch,
afraid to budge from under your rock.

I didn't ask to be lashed up
ready-for-sail, unable to steer
without a man at the wheel.
Given a choice, I would slip
free of this stomach cage
of whalebone stitched into stiff brocade,
no longer a maid but a mermaid
breaking the silver surface.
Being a woman, I don't trouble the glass
with such pictures. I wait for you
to blow the lamp out, for your hands,
in darkness, to draw my figure out.

## Walk with the Groom's Family

We pause, halfway across a spit
cordoning the bay into a dark square,
to watch the tide funneled
through a tiny gate, and to hear,
for the first time clearly, the froth roar.

A lone gull screaks in the wind's mouth
as it whistles and sobs over South
Boston Harbor. It is pleasant
to be chilled to a near deafness,
ears buffed red, with a shell-like lucence,

to see the malachite waves
chip and flake on the mica shore.
Even the pollution glitters: chrome glints
when we peer down from the bridge,
and from the beach, fluted gum wrappers glare.

To the right and to the left
eider ducks dip and float
on the icy surface, delicate
and unperturbed as driftwood.
They consider us— bareheaded,

in wool and leather coats—
but barely ruffle their speckled feathers.
When the first scarlet blotch
of a fever marks the sky,
we turn back. One of my sisters-in-law-

to-be links arm and glove in mine
as the others surge ahead. Now is the time,
as we make the wooden bridge ring
with our heels, to wedge our lives
firmly together, even as our arms crook

and nudge each other's ribs.  This
is the only procession that matters:
our small heads bobbing beneath the wind's wing,
our private selves hurriedly divulged
into the rosy trumpet of the listening ear.

# Dacha Picnic (for Anna and Vladimir Feltzman)

*. . . what woman having ten pieces of silver, if she lose one piece, doth not light a candle, and sweep the house, and seek diligently till she find it?*
Luke 15:8

In the dacha village outside Moscow
trees and bushes are left to grow
wild, cut back only when their wildness
borders on the dangerous. The top
leaves switch in the wind's vague gusts,
lazy as horse tails against the dun-
colored, sunless flank of sky. Anna
greets us at the gate, dressed
entirely in yellow, a mustard seed
that almost smarts. She has an icon's
holy, dire beauty: oval, golden-
lidded eyes. On a wooden table with red legs
she scatters our feast: an enormous
salad and two kinds of bread, an array
of wine and the extraordinary fish,
salmon and sturgeon. Vladimir pours
the vodka and we toast, east and west
tippling a glass in the birchbright cove,
fisting the small, magenta potatoes
from the bowl and eating them
like apples; red wine and lemon vodka
mixed into our voices, gestures. Later,
trampling the spongy, mudsweet pasture
we unnerve a mull-eyed calf into freakish lope.
This season they've named the *belye nochi*:*
afternoon extending as a grace, redolent
as the faded dust lifting from the road.
We return for coffee and cherries
on the porch, nuzzled and quaffed as if
ordinary luxuries. Someone
loses an earring and curses the dark. Outside,
the rasp of low branches, sweeping the dirt.

* belye nochi = *white nights; the midnight sun.*

# Dinner at the Leningrad Train Station

Standing on the street before St. Paul's
Cathedral, a Russian whispers
his name in English. Together, crick-necked,
we endure the golden stare of the icons,
the malachite columns of red and green
shooting up from the floor in a Byzantine
forest. There's something I can do for him:
exchange his rubles for dollars, buy a book
from the hard-currency store. Outside
the tourist shop on Nevsky Prospect he waits
until I return, his third choice, a Japanese
umbrella, tucked under my arm. *Come*, he says,
*and you can eat for free at the station restaurant*
*where I am a waiter*. This is something he can do
for me: a corner table by an open window,
below which a dark crowd slowly mills.
Vladimir brings me *shchi*: cabbage stew
he improves with lamb; sour brown bread,
thin, porous slices he fans
across a plate. Even if I had feasted
for a week — on radishes, cheese, eggs
boiled so long the graygreen yolk
thrusts against the white like a stone —
I'd be every bit as famished, emptied by the faces
whose lives are spent waiting. Out
on the platform, red bulletmarks
of lit cigarettes sear the moving dark.

# The Way the Yellow

The way the yellow gelled on the window
it seemed the three o'clock sun
had cracked in the grass
like a giant egg: yolk-blood sinking
into the lawn, black
shade draped on the wooden dog

house. Ditches and woe pocked the dog
domain: a physical window
on the soul-and-chain. Five black
fungi crouched in roots. One by one sun
beams dropped their lines and sinkers:
strings of honied heat. Along the back fence wild grass

poked from among kempt grass
cousins; a frayed bark from a neighbor's dog.
I poured some milk above the sink,
white drops spilling on the silver rim. Wind
obliquely parted a few wan leaves to let the sun
ooze further still. My brother's black

fingernails pinched the carton closed, his black
hair glinting in the yellow mill. Thin as a grass-
cut, my mother's voice cracked in the sunny
room, *he attacked again; we brought him in; the dog*
*had to be put asleep.* How asleep? The window:
I leaned to see, a small pit sinking

in my throat. Soldered to the quartz-hard sink,
I was stonier. I thought I saw a black
shape move in my disbelief. Through the window
frame a stillness grew, grass
prickled stiff as risen hairs. The dog
too proud for restraint had found escape. Late sun

rifled the treetops with amber hands, sun
light striping the lifeless and live. The sink
held my weight so I hardly flinched, a dog
already running in my head. The new black
ghost uprooted dimpled earth, rolled in grass
and noisily yapped at wrens. A mystical window

yet lingers between us. And a black dog
still leaps when the sun's in the sink.

# Filling the Coop

The small barn looms as we approach, an onyx
envelope propped against the sky. Its quality
of dark, of nighttone, is what sets it off, cuts
it out hard and large from the trees, starglimmer, breeze:
I avoid its black excess as if it rubs off, pitch-
thick, on the palm. Now he tilts, moonsilvered,
against the barndoor edge, rests his full weight
until the whole wall gives, slides open on a darker
tuck, a slit just wide enough to slip through. All
white fades; our teeth bite words without glow.
*Chickens*, he says, rattling a flashlight. The
batteries fall out, thump on the haystrewn planks.
*Needles*, I think, nostrils stitched shut by the
prickly scent, yellow beads I breathe and breathe.
A sudden
beam
leaps from his hand to the ceiling. Overhead,
half a dozen chickens, round with sleep,
make irregular bumps across two thick beams.
One rouses with a scratchy cluck. He is already
broom in hand, motioning toward their cozy lines.
*The trick*, he says, *is to knock them off, cinch
their feet, a few to a hand, and let them hang
faint.* Then we'll carry our odd bouquets
the hundred yards to the wired coop.
Hopeless, of course. I drop the flashlight,
leave its milky band intent on the furthest corner.
The floor is alive with mewling birds. Only when they hang,
head down, can I forget their limp existence;
swing the frightened bulks freely in the pure dark.

## Thaw

*for my sister, two months before my marriage*

Even winter loves this silence; surrenders
to late March with mute twinges
beneath the ice, scars that fracture,
one into another, like the tributaries

of a river. By noon the sun has melted
a hole in the clouds. Yellow
spills across my sister's closed
smile, leaks behind my sunglasses

in a teary stream. Everything blurs
with the changing light: ample pines
lumber up the hill on each other's
heels, the lake a vast black doily

purled with isinglass. Back where we first
stepped out on the ice, a party of men
peer into the circles carved at their feet.
Discarded minnows lie pressed

into the ice around them, flat glints
like coins rolled into pavement.
One man winds the day's catch on his
arm, three silver pouches slit open,

steaming red lining blackening
in air. Already the light drifts out of our hair
like champagne smoke. My sister makes a running
leap and nearly catches her foot

in the small pool between ice and shore.
I choose a place further down,
where the ice is harder, but more
of the lake has seeped into the ground.

# A Letter to Robin Silverman

*On July 30, 1985, a pair of Siberian tigers attacked and killed their zookeeper, Robin Silverman, as she cleaned their cage at the Bronx Zoo's Wild Asia exhibit. A volunteer who accompanied her (and for whom it was the first day on the job) escaped by scaling the 11 ft. fence. Zoo officials stated that Silverman, considered very competent, had violated the 'cardinal rule of animal care' by entering the cage without knowing where the tigers were. Her accidental death was the first in 86 years at the zoo.* —New York Times, *July 30*

*Correction: Officials said today that Silverman's chores had not included cleaning the tiger cage that day.* —New York Times, *July 31*

Though such a death is not easily
conceived as chosen, I often imagine you
standing there: skillful fingers hesitant
for an instant on the gate's lock; the flatly

insistent morning light awash on your face;
how, in its pale, high relief, your assistant
must have seen minute hairs, fine as new fur, prickling
across your cheeks. Had she known, what else

might she have seen; rigid intent in a sidelong glance,
a warning flush as you let yourself in? Trust
is reckless, a human trait; at the last moment
she saw, with ferocious clarity, your terrible mistake,

bristling at the alien pleasure of close range.
Beneath the greenblack cover of imported brush, two pairs
of eyes opened like glittery flowers as nostrils
quivered awake; tails wagged in lazy crescents.

Wild Asia was spurred to instinct.
However I choose to understand what brought
you to the fence, I bring my own hand
up to the latch. There are no cardinal rules

in the treatment of one human by another. In the teeming air
of our narrow escapes, we freely observe our species
advance, capable and composed, toward
extinction, increasingly eager

for what must appear,
as it approaches, more beautiful
and superior
with every step.

*Followed by Children Who Threw Stones*

# Topsham Farm

There are no knobs, only latches
to open or bolt the doors. This farmhouse,
damp in the marrow of its boards, is over
two hundred years old. It looms
on the hill, an enormous saxifrage
unburdening boxy flowers on a stony slope.
This place is not my home, but I love
the red front door as if I had painted it myself.

~

I think of the goats as philosophers: Plato, Kant;
Pans without the manly chest; old men
with hoary whiskers, muttering my rudest thoughts
deep into thicketed beards. The associations,
of course, are wrong. With each shovel of pungent
granola into the trough at dinnertime, the she-goats
butt each other's backsides, diseased udders
jostling between their legs, round
with tainted milk. I spill
three mounds on the ruinous straw
rather than endure their witches' tongues.

Feeding, I can see the female:
gypsy-beauties, they poke long chins
into the air to watch me, chewing thoughtfully
and deliberately with small, even teeth,
horns twisted up like kerchief knots,
clear eyes brown and goldflecked.
Once, blue jeans tucked inside high black boots,
I descended into their pen to touch them. Fear
was milky on their breaths. Up close,
their agate eyes aroused my own fear,
the slits opening up and shutting like doors.

~

The female Dalmatian, Heidi, is deaf,
that is, listens to my face: the quirky

language of brow and lip. Languid nymph
of the watery eyes, she trails my progress
around house and farm, lies down beside me
fluent as a shadow; nightly clambers
onto the bed to guard the gates
of my fitful sleep. This much closeness
with a human would revolt me: cold nose
burrowed into my neck, sharp ribs
shelved against mine, the weedy fragrance
of her beseeching tongue. Though I smack
her hind to shoo her away, it is with
little conviction.

~

Dawn unswathes the trees, stripping the dark gauze
with clammy fingers. The horses wake
me with their guttural chatter,
kneading the cool earth with their hooves
until the dust rises like flour.
They are clannish and doleful
but not unfriendly. They nuzzle the air
while I break another bale
into washtubs heaped with their vitamined meal.

Once, late with the five o'clock dinner,
I gropingly plucked tubs from between their hooves,
shivering in the ankle-high dew. Their animal bodies
steamed and chugged like invisible engines,
dinosaur-enormous and touchingly helpless.
I stood a long time by the fence,
listening to the barbarous lullaby of food.

~

Rain confines me to the house,
where I limit myself to the horsehair
couch, ruptured at the seams
with ancient stuffing. I develop
a rash if I read too long.

Late this afternoon the clouds clapped shut,
the farm wrung out by a burst of sun.
Icy beads flash in the grass, a plum-
saffron band cinching the horizon.

The chicken coop comes alive with pent-up
frustration, when, foot first, I enter
with a bucket. They squawk and claw
for the grain, pecking at my ankles.
One hen, queen of the harem, gores her own egg
as I lift it up from between her legs,
her beak lassoed with the ropy white.
I kick her, hard. Some of the yolk
comes away on my palm, crumbled
shell glued to my skin.

~

When I stand at the edge, it seems impossible
that my bedroom window also holds this field,
locks four bars around its sweeping color, gentle
drift of valley into hill, a tiny, Titian world
grafted into the wall. The wind lifts, pinksilver
with dragonfly, milkweed, thistle and clover,
while the field's one tune plays over and over:
fife-toned peepers warbling in the brook, fiddler
katydids, the vulgar whisk and whistle of seed.

If I am led by anything, it is the *sotto voce*
of the trees, the original wind instruments whose
concert I breathe. All summer I've drowsed
to their eerie air, woken to a sound like my name
being called. Once I might have stopped my ears,
afraid of the words that rustle the leaves.
Now I throw the shutters wide, my hair about
my neck like a shawl, alert for the enchanted pitch
that draws, and will draw me away from here.

# Lobster Tank, New York Deli

This is no place for a duel, the cramped new sea
where you glide over the rust-colored body
of your friend. The way you flail the filter's
mouth makes the bubbles leak out, faster, whiter,
your claws powerless as barnacled swords against
the invisible foe. Oh, but you're handsome, pirate:
your leathery skin gleams with booty. You'd rather
jig on a plank than reform your ways, rather
go kicking to your grave than sink
as your cellmates have. This city is an ark,
whose swelling deck holds scores of every living
creature; if you were the last lobster on the earth
we would strip your tiny hull beyond even
the notion of its worth.

# The Pelican in Its Piety

Symbolic, the Middle-Aged world
believes, the way the pelican feeds
its young: the chicks drenched
with what looks like blood,

a sour mash the mother returns, half-digested,
from her bill; notes how both sexes
guard the brood, pitching their huge striped
wings like tents about the chicks

who, pushing up on their own
creased fans, pitchfork the nest
when they tumble down. It is possible, then,
to perceive morality in the simplest

terms: on the Nile, where the pelican
lives, a punishing sun pelts the palms'
fringed canopy, the random beams
falling through the roof, searing

as Hell's raining coal.
On learning that the chicks rebel,
with a flurry of wings and bills
jabbed in their parents' faces,

the scholars, who equate these creatures with
pious devotion, know the parents are right to
kill, twisting the necks of the offspring who
would otherwise peck them to death.

For three days the nest is silent,
a spiced breeze bending the canopy.
Then, in a wide lazy
rush of wings, the mother pelican

returns. In a perfect example of piety
she bends over the nest, a terrific wound
opening on her breast and the 'life-blood'
pours forth; the errant children revive, to be

lavished again by their doting parents.
Devotion, death and resurrection. Plain as
day what it must mean to the bestiarian: clearing his
throat, he dictates to the scribes

hunched over their desks the obvious
parallel between pelicans and Christ,
absolving the terrible sacrifices
required of the child.

# Honeymoon Cruise

Eastward, where a blazing sun had promised to rise
over Mount Desert Isle,

a silver dawn lit the horizon. I wore
one of your heaviest sweaters, wished for

gloves, felt the boat pitch
as we climbed aboard. Someone had strung the vessel with

decorative buoys and nets,
leaving a mound of grimy lifejackets

piled up like shipwrecks against the prow.
Fifteen miles out, while spumy thunderclouds

blew in from the south, our guide spoke, pointing at
the gray waves that drew our boat

forward. Here, he assured
us, whales had been spotted; now, all that was required

was our patience. I'll
never forget the curve of your smile

as we huddled
in silence, the visibility as if we peered

through gray silk. My own face
was hooked with annoyance

at our having been taken for a ride.
It was a relief when we turned back with the tide,

heading home
in a blinding July rain.

You made light
of it

as we neared shore, pointing out
seals and birds, getting your money's worth, while I felt

the steely wash of disappointment
douse the day, refusing to believe until we'd docked that

something incomparably vast
might not, at the last

moment, rise.

# Digging

All week, as we honeymoon
along the puzzle-piece coastline of Maine,

scratching our names into sand white
and flecked

as birchbark, picking across one beach in darkness
where the driftwood gleams like eerie phosphorous,

the horseshoe crab eludes our notice;
burrowing as we pause

to squint after osprey and cormorant,
or pluck at our reflections, where snails bed with hermit

crabs. Only on our last day he appears, washing up
like a helmet on the waves. What catches my heart

is the way his armored bulk suddenly begins to
move, too fast for my fingers to

pinch; the curious attraction I feel
for the disdainful

way he erases himself. I turn him gently
over, touch the vulnerable underbelly

he has labored to hide from me. In a few
hours we will enter a new

life together. Survival makes his tiny tail
swipe, midair; the reason we return to the sea

the hideous creature we regard as beautiful.

# The Artist's Palette

I'll be the first, Red says
to Yellow, not *you*, tart
lemon brassy
sass canary,
so just keep your electric
school bus lies to yourself!

So much for the razz a ma tazz.

Oh, you can bellow, Yellow
don't think I haven't heard you:
Texas rose
and Black-
eyed Susan; you so stunning in amber
saffron dandelion
topaz!
Sing to me you pretty
Siren; I dig
that ochre-ache.

~

Miserable scut! Why does the harlot
dress in scarlet?
O fevered flame, o
titian tint,
how many beauties 'baptised'
in your sanguine depths?

Isn't sin a grin, a red-
letter day? One need only jump
in
to become cardinal carmine ma
genta vermillion. Why, you're a regular Brick,

a bruise for my lips, my cherry
berry pimp! You make me sick o ruby

rube. Beware the pomegranate prince,
ladies: my gold was sold for six of his seeds.

~

Says Blue, Seems you're both confused.
Let's not gild the lily *or* rose.
There has only ever been
the paradigm of my indigo:
a cool blackblue to bathe the night
and taffy pulled to flat azure
by Day — a cerrulean quilt
strewn with white rosettes. Every spring I infuse
the new: hyacinth and robin's egg,
the bellflowers by my name. Dive
into my eyes for the ultra in aqua
marine. I am everywhere at once:
a fresh snow prinked with sapphire glints,
a maudlin tune you stop to sing.
The jolt behind electric, plus,
I wash the poet's soul.

## St. Andrews, Firth of Forth

My last day in that Scottish town
I walked my bike down
Market Street, past mechants nodding
to their wares as they smoked,
the men's thumbs clothespinning
their shirt-sleeved elbows

and the women in kerchiefs:
paisley prints, to hawk spring
with; under the archway graven with a king's
image, and under the long withered arms of the tree
planted by Mary,
Queen of Scots; hurrying

now, past gardens kindling
with cockleshell-pink roses, and along
the East Sands, the bike quailing
under my weight when I charged
the hill to Kinkell Braes.
The town shrank as I walked the cliffs:

a jagged starfish, gray spires
nubbing its sand-red skin;
cathedral and castle ruins
on two of its points —
hope chests half unpacked
of their heirloom contents — and a two-tiered pier

laid like an oar
on the North Sea. Squinting,
I could make out fishermen
hauling and sinking their lobster trap
rosaries, boat masts doodling
in the long shadow of the pier.

Now was the hour for dear
grannies to gather in the old tea houses.
The tide was going out when I leaned
to look: gulls and plovers frisked

the rocks, diving in the
green-white

smash. Here, the cliff ended in a jut,
falling away on one side into a rocky beach,
and on it, twin, extinguished volcanoes,
one named Maiden, the other, Rock
and Spindle. I climbed
down, carefully.

Lava, filed by the tide's changing, seemed freshly
stalled: eruptions no less vehement
for all their salty centuries
of cooling. The town
was a distant flash
I had to walk into the waves to see;

what betrayal that it could all go on without me,
my friends, all the life in that speck . . .
All go on? the cliffs in answer
rumbled loudly. I turned:
the sea was still, the volcanoes still
cold. I scrambled back up. A herd

of black cows, broken loose, raced
like brush fire across the field
to the cliff: buckling, at the edge,
to a stop. Mauve
and amethyst, dust from their path
now slowly rose

up in a cloud of gauze —
hypnotizing, unifying the outlaws —
while a mush-lump
chewed in the collective
unconscious
passed, in an

instant, from horn
to horn: a rank
familiar odor trembling
on the wind, wind
of safe return and
the other world.

# EverGlade

This is the green the world was born in —
pungently lush, heady with moss
    and ferment, the mealy underside of bark
and what creeps along the vine in rain —
oozing sap-pores, wrinkled cobwebs, palm oil, musk

and Venus-hair. Not spring's yellow-emerald
but a more pregnant jungle-green
    dresses the glade,
every leaf and flower straining to reach
the thin-as-a-newt's-tail strands of sunlight
    that brush

palm and coconut's cowlick bangs,
    their shingled
    teenager
    trunks,
down to the waterlogged stumps
rotting along every path.
It is not enough

to be tough as rubber, spongy and brilliant,
    dappled and striped:
tunneling roots that pummel
the soil
as they grow, or the 'roots' air carries — spores —
    are required;

the muscular fingers of the mangrove tree,
whose branches grow shoots
    that take root,
until a passel of new trunks knit
the mother-fist in an open-the-door, see-

all-the-people bower. The air is a kind of floating water
that steams freely off the real water,
escaping like fossil gas from a tomb
    decay and death's
burgeoning, untapped excesses.

What a riot of emotion the red
    rubber plant arouses,
stuck out like a tongue
    beside a palm's quilted
bark. The salamander instinctively eschews
its shelter. And

here, heckled by a hidden macaw,
how rightly aloof the snowy egret
as he preens his foot,
splaying the claws,

eyes
primed for the tiny blips
the minnows'
shadows

make. What else may we believe
    when, in a downpour
that bends
the fronds and sends
the peacocks undercover,

from among a logjam
    of drowsy gators
a gold-mailed knight
half-mounts the bank, his snout
Excalibur's

sword released,
  but
  that
      enchantment
  exists?

# The Day God Made the Peacock

he was thinking
of something else. The first blue burst
of ocean, perhaps, as he dreamed the feathered neck:
miles of unearthly hue unbroken by wave or whitecap.
These might have been enough for a lesser god —
a throat rare as a blue moon, the crown of three gold
tufts — but evil yet slithered in the murk
of his thoughts. So the peacock's head swivels
on its elegant muscle, a snake unfurled
from turquoise flames. Whether he glimpsed or heard
his mottled cats, he stitched their dazzling coats
onto the peacock's back, let the patterns mix
and shirr by jungle. This being done, God slept
the fractured sleep of an artist loathe to admit
creative impasse. The air was yellow
with unfed schemes. As evening touched fire to the bay,
at the point where sun and water make each other
green, he opened his eyes to the sea. Alone
with the eerie crackle of the flames, the whole sky
gone up in exquisite smoke — teal, ochre, plum
jade — God wept and multiplied his joy, row
upon row in the creature's tail. And was proud.

# The Bones of Potter's Field

We have fired so long in this great wide
kiln the clay is bleached with our calcium
our skulls reshaped into cups and handles
our knees cracked bowls our hips halved jugs.
When they bear down with their shovels to dig
another in, the rich sand turning over
the way leaves turn over in the wind, whole
dark slices rain with knuckles. In the field
to bury strangers in, out of our newly
gleaming bones we assemble the One who
will rise again.

## Followed by Children Who Threw Stones

On his daily walk to the studio, M. Cezanne's
ordinary apples bulged like genitals
in his front coat pockets. He'd rise
with the milkblue spill of dawn,
coarse cloth drawn over gooseflesh,

and inhale with his five rapacious senses
the bruised return of the Auvers sun.
Children, returning from their chores,
pelted his form with fruit
and stones, in hopes of some obscene

and sparkling oath, the furious thrill
of his shaking fist or hand,
oversized and lobster-bronze, raised
to protect his hairless dome. There was almost
a comfort in this, their ritual of hate

and faithful ignorance, wearing
the same faces of the Parisian critics.
In one letter he wrote: 'I am still
learning'; only his wife
and the local gardener would consent

to sit for him. Other things had no choice:
wine bottles, borrowed blankets, lemons
and conchs.
                    Today, I walk through one pocket
of the city I live in, hoping to love or believe
the things I find. Crowds surge and bellow

in a dozen languages. One man instructs,
at the top of his lungs, the reasons why Jesus
had to die for us. I am thirsty to distraction
and so, standing before the open bins, reach
for the hardheartedness of apples like his.

## *Anhinga Prize for Poetry*

| **Selection:** | **Judge:** |
|---|---|
| Jean Monahan<br>*Hands* | 1991<br>Donald Hall |
| (no winner) | 1990<br>Denise Levertov |
| Nick Bozanic<br>*The Long Drive Home* | 1989<br>Judith Hemschemeyer |
| Julianne Seeman<br>*Enough Light to See* | 1988<br>Charles Wright |
| Will Wells<br>*Conversing with the Light* | 1987<br>Henry Taylor |
| Robert Levy<br>*The Whistle Maker* | 1986<br>Robin Skelton |
| Judith Kitchen<br>*Perennials* | 1985<br>Hayden Carruth |
| Sherry Rind<br>*The Hawk in the Back Yard* | 1984<br>Louis Simpson |
| Ricardo Pau-Llosa<br>*Sorting Metaphors* | 1983<br>William Stafford |